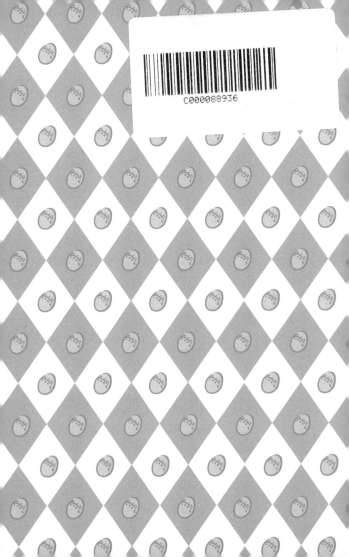

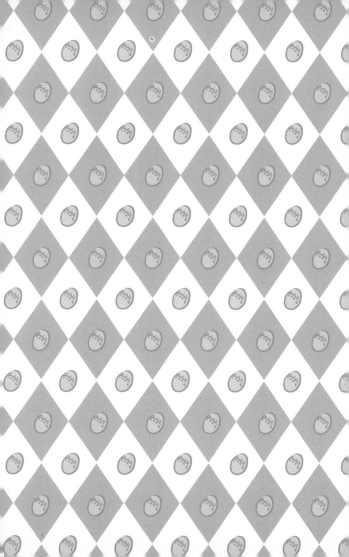

Cricket's

FUNNIEST
JOKES

Jim Chumley

summersdale

CRICKET'S FUNNIEST JOKES

Copyright © Summersdale Publishers Ltd, 2009

Illustrations by Robert Duncan

Summersdale Publishers Ltd
46 West Street
Chichester
West Sussex
PO19 1RP
UK

www.summersdale.com

Printed and bound by Tien Wah Press

ISBN: 978-1-84024-747-3

Substantial discounts on bulk quantities of Summersdale books are available to corporations, professional associations and other organisations. For details telephone Summersdale Publishers on (+44-1243-771107), fax (+44-1243-786300) or email (nicky@summersdale.com).

Cricket's

FUNNIEST
JOKES

Jim Chumley

Editor's Note

According to Douglas Adams, cricket is 'generally regarded as an incomprehensibly dull and pointless game'. Pointless maybe, but dull? This compilation of the cream of cricketing jokes begs to differ.

Anyone who happens to play the gentleman's game will strike a rich comedic vein given the unlikely characters that constitute a cricket team. Fielders have plenty of time to think up gags both on and off the pitch. As for blundering bowlers, unctuous umpires, belligerent batsmen and wise-cracking wicketkeepers – the jokes just write themselves.

These pages are packed with quotes and quips from those who know the game best – it's guaranteed to crease you up!

Completely Batty

What does a drunk cricketer have
in common with a good bat?

They're both well oiled.

Arrogant batsman: **There are three players on this team who are too rubbish even to be selected.**

Captain: **Could you point out the other two, please?**

There was an industrial dispute during a test match at Lord's.

The batsmen were the first union to come out on a non-strike.

A batsman received a dressing down by the captain for being bowled out after an easy ball.

'Very well,' said the player, 'how should I have played the shot?'

'Under an assumed name,' said the wicketkeeper.

'It's a great pity you didn't take the game up sooner,' said one batsman to his older partner, who had just accidentally run him out.

'Do you mean I'd be playing first class cricket by now?' asked his partner.

'No,' replied the batsman. 'I mean you would have already retired!'

'Has the home team scored a run yet?' enquired the spectator arriving late to the game.

'Don't ask me,' replied the man. 'I've only been watching them for the last two years.'

Two spectators were
watching the local match.

'That batsman was really late for
the first delivery,' noted one.

'He always is,' said the other.
'He's the milkman.'

Which is the only animal you
should take on to a cricket pitch?

A bat.

What happened to the batsman
who held up his end all afternoon?

He got terrible cramp.

The captain wanted to know why the batsman was out in the first over.

'The ball came back very quickly,' he explained.

'Not quite as quickly as you!' retorted the captain.

**What does an Australian
cricketer look like?**

Tanned, slim, holding the Ashes…

Wicketkeeper: Your bat's just like a doughnut.

Batsman: Why, because I always hit the sweet spot with it?

Wicketkeeper: No, because it seems to have a hole in it.

'I can't really say I'm batting badly. I'm not batting long enough to be batting badly.'

GREG CHAPPELL, FORMER AUSTRALIAN CRICKETER

'I batted the best score of my life today!' said Toby.

'Never mind,' replied Ben. 'Don't let that put you off.'

The mayor was being shown around a prison where a cricket match was being played.

'That batsman's got talent,' he said, 'what's he in for?'

'Hit and run!' replied the warder.

Bowled Over

Why did the bat make
the cricketer cry?

It was made of weeping willow.

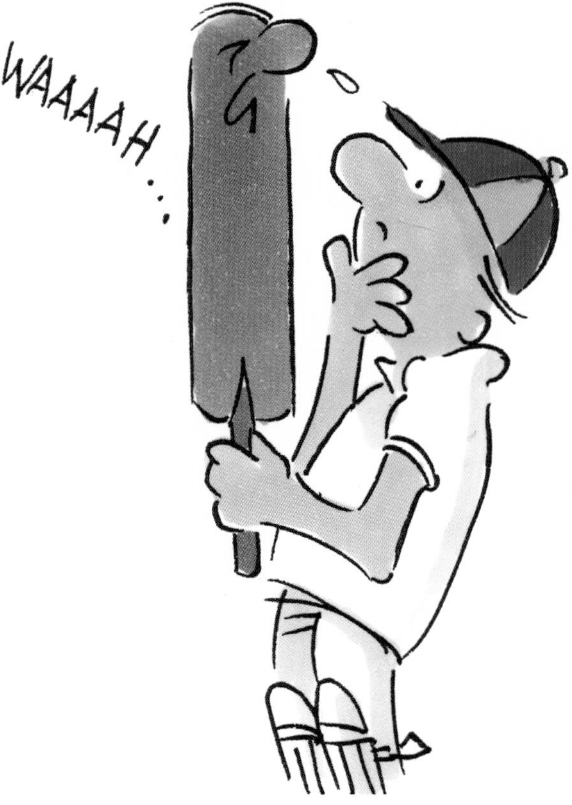
WAAAAAH...

The bowler hit the batsman in the face with the ball and broke three of his teeth. The batsman went for treatment, and then bravely walked back on.

'Don't worry,' shouted the bowler. 'I'll aim for the stumps this time!'

'They asked me how I'd like to play for England,' said John.

'"Really badly" I said.'

'I should think you could manage that,' replied Sophie. 'All the other players seem to.'

Bowler: I'd like to stand
for a test, please.

Captain: Sorry, we don't accept
new people standing.

Bowler: How can I get a test, then?

Captain: Beg on your knees.

Blame It on the Umpire

God and the Devil agreed
to have a cricket match.

God thought he would win,
because there were lots of Test
batsmen and bowlers in Heaven.

But he overlooked the fact that
all the umpires lived in Hell.

Batsmen run after the shot.
Fielders run after the ball.
Umpires run after the match.

What do cricketers do when
they lose their eyesight?

Become umpires.

'You can't trust anyone these days,'
complained Bill after the match.

'Why do you say that?'
asked Philip.

'Well,' replied Bill, 'I bribed
the umpire this afternoon
and we still lost!'

'Where are your glasses?' protested the dismissed batsman angrily to the man wearing the white coat and hat. 'I think you're the one who needs glasses,' replied the man, 'but perhaps you would like to buy an ice cream?'

All Out!

'Good morning's work for me,'
said the cricket-loving dentist,
feeling pleased with himself. 'I
had them all out before lunch!'

'There's nothing wrong with being aggressive – the bloke down the other end has a bat, some pads and a helmet.'

SIMON JONES

The streaker ran through the ladies' changing room and disappeared out of the door.

'Was that a regular member?' asked one, shocked.

'A little on the small side, if you ask me,' replied another.

The young man got permission to take the day off so he could be at his father's funeral. His boss was furious to see the man at the local cricket match that very afternoon. When he arrived the score was 0 for 6.

'This doesn't look like your father's funeral to me!' fumed the boss.

'I wouldn't be too sure,' the man gulped, 'he's next up to bat!'

'I had five catches dropped this afternoon,' complained the bowler.

'True,' replied his skipper. 'But the spectators aren't expected to catch them from all the way up in the stands…!'

'I bowl so slow that if after
I have delivered the ball I
don't like the look of it, I can
run after it and bring it back.'

J. M. BARRIE

Creasing Up

Why do cricketers look
weather-beaten?

Because rain always stops play.

'I've never played such a
terrible innings before.'

'So, you've played before, then?'

'There was a slight
interruption there
for athletics.'

RICHIE BENAUD, REFERRING TO A STREAKER AT LORD'S

'Now, don't forget to get behind the ball,' said the coach to the boy.

'But it's round!' the boy exclaimed. 'How do you tell which is the front and which is the back?'

A fielder on the boundary ran to make a catch deep in the field, but he stumbled and the ball fell through his hands.

'I could probably have caught that quite easily in my mouth,' jeered a spectator.

'If my mouth was as enormous as yours, I probably could have done too,' snapped the fielder.

Captain: Are you any good
at wicket-keeping?

Applicant: Passable.

Captain: We've got one like that.
I want one that's impassable!

One cricketer asked another, 'Does
your village boast a cricket team?'

'We have a team,' replied the
other. 'But I wouldn't say it was
anything to boast about!'

The cricket team were losing very heavily and couldn't decide which batsman to play next.

'Shall we bring out our hooker?' asked one player.

'The game's not over yet, young man, we'll have none of that,' replied the captain.

The wicketkeeper had a bad day, dropping eight catches. What's more, he felt a bit under the weather. 'I've got a cold coming on,' he muttered.

'Well, it makes a change that you've been able to catch something,' grumbled the bowler.

Oddballs

'I don't go as far as that
on my holidays.'

Caught out early, the batsman made his way to the pavilion for his lunch of fish and chips. 'This batter's terrible,' he grimaced.

The chef scowled back, 'Look who's talking!'

The police arrived at the match.

'We've had a report of an individual acting suspiciously, loitering around without doing anything,' said the sergeant.

'Oh yes, he's over there,' replied the groundsman, pointing to the England fielder.

Who scores a hat-trick?

A bowler, of course!

Simply Not Cricket

'The English are not very
spiritual people, so they
invented cricket to give
them some idea of eternity.'

G. B. SHAW

How is blind optimism defined?

An England batsman
applying suntan lotion.

Bowler: I've got a brilliant idea
for improving our team.

Captain: Excellent! When
will you be leaving?

The batsman, proud of his sporting prowess, was keen to impress his mother-in-law sitting in the stands. Taking his position on the crease, he turned to the wicketkeeper and said, 'I plan to really belt this one. My mother-in-law is over there.'

'Don't be daft,' replied the wicketkeeper. 'You'll never hit her at this distance!'

'I couldn't bat for the length of time required to score 500. I'd get bored and fall over.'

DENNIS COMPTON

A bout of torrential rain had cast doubts on whether a crucial Test match would take place. The ground was soaked, but they decided to play anyway. The home captain won the toss and, after a moment's thought, exclaimed, 'Right then – we'll have the shallow end.'

Why did the cricket team sack the committee at their village show?

They said it was time to take charge of their own fete.

'I'm surprised the spectators don't riot out of boredom!' said one bowler to the other during the dull match.

'Yes, but it's difficult to shout and yawn at the same time,' replied his friend.

When do Sussex batsmen display their best footwork?

When they walk back to the pavilion.

Wrong Footed

'I just want to get into
the middle and get the
right sort of runs.'

Robin Smith, South African cricketer, on suffering
from diarrhoea while on tour in India

What's worse than wearing a
cold box from your sports bag?

Wearing a warm box
from someone else's.

'If W. G. Grace were here today
I wonder how he would play in
this Twenty20 cricket match?'

'Not very well I shouldn't
think. He'd be over one
hundred and fifty years old!'

'If the fans start haranguing me for my autograph,' said the arrogant county player, 'I pretend that I don't play any more.'

Said the journalist under his breath, 'I'm not sure you have to pretend.'

'Where's your scoreboard?' asked the visiting captain.

'Over there,' said the home bowler, pointing to a strapping boxer standing by the pavilion.

'What if we don't agree with his scoring?' asked the visiting captain.

'You can take it up with him afterwards,' offered the local bowler.

Which cricket team is most sensibly dressed for cold weather?

The Vest Indies.

A new cricket stadium was built in outer space.

It was terrible – there was no atmosphere at all.

'How can I improve my batting?'

'You need to play with
more spirit, son.'

'I've had three vodkas and a gin
already – I won't be able to see
the ball if I have any more.'

'Do you know the statistics for last season?' a cricketer asked at his club's annual general meeting.

'Well, as far as I know, it was 298 gallons of beer in 50 pubs.'

Down But Not Out

Patient: Doctor, I'm feeling
just like an umpire.

Doctor: Don't be silly.
There must be someone
somewhere who likes you!

Patient: **Doctor, I think I'm a cricket bail!**

Doctor: **Feeling a bit off, are you?**

One cricketer to another:

That doctor doesn't know what he's talking about.

What did he say?

He told me I've got tennis elbow!

Patient: **Doctor, I've got a cricket bat in my ear!**

Doctor: **How's that?**

Patient: **Don't start that again!**

Patient: **Doctor, I think
I'm a cricket ball!**

Doctor: **Don't worry,
it'll be over soon.**

Batsman: **My doctor has told
me I can't play cricket.**

Captain: **I didn't know he
knew you so well!**

The umpire bent his arm
and shouted, 'One short.'

'Cheeky!' replied the batsman.
'How did you know?'

Patient: Doctor, I keep seeing ducks before my eyes.

Doctor: Have you seen an optician?

Patient: No, just ducks.

Hit and Mrs

'What do you think about Joan
going off with the cricket coach?'

'I didn't know she could drive.'

A batsman saw his friend moping around behind the pavilion at the end of a match and asked him why he looked so despondent.

'My wife has told me she wants a divorce,' he said glumly.

'Really?' enquired his friend, 'On what grounds?'

'Oh, I'm not sure; it could be Headingley, Lord's, Edgbaston...'

'I've just got a new cricket bat for my husband.'

'Wow, what a great swap!'

'Doctor, I need something to help my husband rest before his big match.'

'Here are some sleeping pills. They should do the trick.'

'What's the dosage?'

'You just swallow half of them this evening and he'll be right as rain in the morning.'

'The wife says that if I don't stop playing cricket she'll leave me.'

'Oh dear! That's too bad.'

'Yes, I'll miss her.'

'Pitches are like wives – you can never tell how they're going to turn out.'

LEONARD HUTTON

Fred always played cricket on Sunday. This troubled his wife, so she asked the vicar whether it was a sin to play on Sunday.

'It's not a sin,' replied the vicar. 'The way he plays, it's a *crime!*'

Smith took his wife to a cricket match and, although bored, she sat patiently through the first innings. During the second, a batsman made a wild hook and cleared the ball from the grounds. 'Thank goodness they got rid of it,' said Smith's wife, 'Now we can all go home.'

Have you enjoyed this book? If so, why not write a review on your favourite website? Thanks very much for buying this Summersdale book.

www.summersdale.com

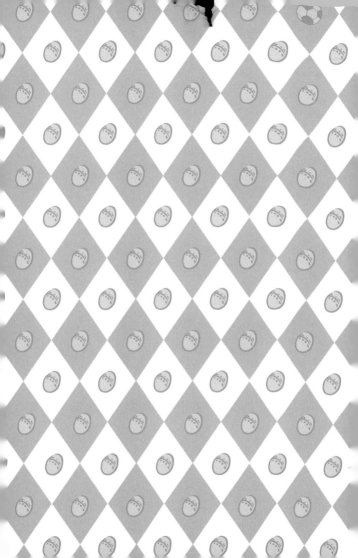

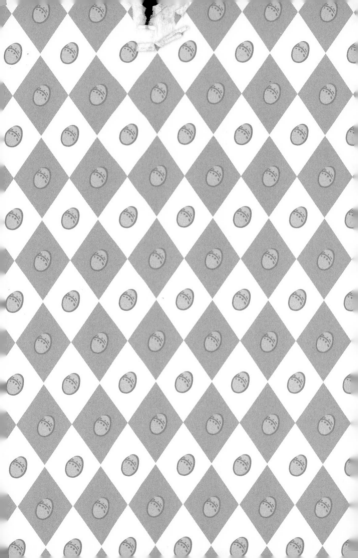